PENGUIN BOOKS

P.W. BOTHA
IN HIS OWN WORDS

Pieter-Dirk Uys was born in Cape Town, South Africa, in 1945. He has written over 30 plays and revues that have been performed throughout South Africa and abroad. He is known for his impersonation of P.W. Botha on stage.

P.W. BOTHA
IN HIS OWN WORDS

COMPILED BY PIETER-DIRK UYS

PENGUIN BOOKS

Penguin Books Ltd, Harmondsworth, Middlesex, England
Viking Penguin Inc., 40 West 23rd Street, New York, New York 10010, U.S.A.
Penguin Books Australia Ltd, Ringwood Victoria, Australia
Penguin Books Canada Ltd, 2801 John Street Markham, Ontario, Canada L3R IB4
Penguin Books (N.Z.) Ltd, 82-190 Wairau Road, Auckland 10, New Zealand
Penguin South Africa, 20 Skietlood Street, Isando

First published 1987

Typeset by Cityset
Printed by Printpak Books, Dacres Avenue, Epping, Cape
Set 10 on 12 pt Plantin

The name of Dimitri Tsafendas comes to mind, without whom we might still be deep into the reign of Emperor Hendrik the First.

GLOSSARY

AWB: Afrikaner Weerstandbeweging (Afrikaner Resistance Movement)

HNP: Herstigte Nasionale Party (Re-established National Party)

House of Assembly: White Chamber of Parliament

House of Representatives: Coloured Chamber of Parliament

House of Delegates: Indian Chamber of Parliament

CP: Conservative Party

ANC: African National Congress

PFP: Progressive Federal Party

Info Scandal: Unauthorised activities by Department of Information in the 1970s

NP: National Party

SWAPO: South West African Peoples' Organisation

SWA: South West Africa, also called Namibia, Trust Territory originally mandated to South Africa by the League of Nations after World War I

ACKNOWLEDGEMENTS

Having often been accused, through my impersonations of our present State President PW Botha, of being responsible for the general state of our land, allow me to put the record straight and give full credit to the man himself. It has always been my intention (and I have done so often in the past), to acknowledge the South African Government as my scriptwriters.

This collection of quotations drawn from speeches, interviews and statements prove my point.

Among those I would like to thank, other than Mrs Elize Botha for keeping her husband in such good nick for so long, and the white voters of South Africa who put him where he is today, a special thanks to Sheila Watt and her staff at *The Star* Library Johannesburg for being so helpful.

Thanks also to the relatively free press of yesteryear for reporting what he said and the censored press of today for still reporting what he says.

P-D.U.

Pieter Willem Botha is the first Executive State President of the Republic of South Africa. He is the Leader of the ruling National Party.

The results of the most recent parliamentary elections that returned him to power are as follows:

Out of 3 027 519 registered white voters, 2 057 811 voted. The National Party took 52,4% of the vote, the Conservative Party 26,37% and the Progressive Federal Party 14,11%.

There are 29 443 614 persons in South Africa, according to the preliminary 1985 census figures, including the self-governing states and homelands:

Blacks	21 197 253	who have no representation in Parliament
Asian	801 758	who are represented in the House of Delegates
Coloured	2 853 964	who are represented in the House of Representatives
White	4 590 639	who are represented in the House of Assembly

P.W. Botha was born in the district of Paul Roux in the Orange Free State on 12 January 1916. Married, with five children.

1946	Appointed Union Information Officer of the National Party, as well as Secretary of the 'Nasionale Jeugbond' (Youth Action).
1946-48	In charge of the publicity campaign of the National Party in all four provinces.
1948-58	Chief Secretary of the National Party in the Cape Province.
1948	Elected Member of Parliament for George in the Cape.
1958-61	Deputy Minister of the Interior.
1961	Minister of Community Development and Coloured Relations.
1964	Also becomes Minister of Public Works.
1966	Appointed Minister of Defence and elected leader of the National Party in the Cape Province.
1975	Appointed Leader of the House of Assembly.
1978	Becomes the eighth Prime Minister of South Africa, retaining also the portfolios of Defence and National Security.
1984	Becomes the first Executive State President

'I was 20 when I started in politics.'

**London *Sunday Times* Magazine
29 March 1987**

'I hope I am 70 years young and not old.'

**On his 70th birthday from his holiday
home at The Wilderness to *The Citizen*
13 January 1987**

'Also, English is not my natural language, I express myself better in Afrikaans.'

London *Sunday Times* Magazine
29 March 1987

'I try to be a man of peace, but if people tempt me I can become a Thunderbird.'

As State President
House of Representatives
19 August 1987

'Stay, join hands with us and help us make South Africa a great and prosperous nation. It is still the best country in the world to live in.'

As Minister of Defence, to those leaving S.A.
At meeting in George
1 November 1976

'Make no mistake, we have guts. South Africa is a valuable jewel defended by determined men.'

**As State President in interview
with Paris *Figaro*
The Star 8 December 1986**

'In no country of the world is there more dedicated striving for better relations between peoples.'

**As Minister of Defence, Republic Day
celebrations in Potchefstroom
24 May 1976**

'Ours is a great responsibility and South Africa is a shining example of stability.'

**As Minister of Defence
Robertson 3 May 1975**

'We are a strong country in a rather sick world.'

**As Prime Minister, in US
'Business Week' interview
Sunday Express 4 April 1982**

'South Africa is guarding a very important access route between the East and the West, and we also possess some of the world's largest reserves of strategic metals.'

**As Minister of Defence, opening the new airport
at Vereeniging, Transvaal
1 June 1977**

'In a relatively short span of years our problems will to a large extent be behind us.'

**As Prime Minister, NP Congress Durban
15 August 1979**

'Where in the whole wide world today can you find a more just society than South Africa has?'

**As Minister of Defence,
House of Assembly 6 May 1976**

'We are probably no better, but certainly no worse than the rest of the world.'

**As State President,
NP Congress Durban 12 August 1986**

'If a foreign visitor comes to South Africa ordinary decency would force us to receive him properly.'

**As State President, in Paris, after being snubbed
by the French government during his visit
to Delville Wood Memorial
12 November 1986**

'Many refugees – White, Brown and Black – flee to South Africa. Why? Here they know they have safety.'

**As Minister of Defence,
East London NP Congress
1 September 1975**

'We will outlive [pressure on South Africa] and will eventually succeed in becoming a haven of rest.'

**As Prime Minister, receiving honorary
citizenship of Kroonstad
17 November 1980**

'South Africa is not a jellyfish and is in many respects a swordfish.'

**As State President, House of Assembly
28 April 1986**

'A person who does nothing makes no mistakes.'

London *Sunday Times* **Magazine**
29 March 1987

'No Prime Minister before me has been attacked more viciously than I am today.'

As State President, Election Meeting
Pietermaritzburg 30 April 1987

'It is not a job that anyone should apply for.'

Referring to the job of Prime Minister on the
eve of his election as such.
Interview _The Star_ 30 September 1978

'I am presented by my enemies and my opponents as being very strict and despotic, an evil being. That is not so.'

London _Sunday Times_ Magazine 29 March 1987

'I am not bound by any chains to my present position.'

London _Sunday Times_ Magazine 29 March 1987

'I once told parliament that I can think of a lot of things I would rather do.'

London _Sunday Times_ Magazine 29 March 1987

'I am in the hands of those who elected me. As long as I have the confidence of people and they call upon me to stay, surely I will stay.'

As State President on: would he retire?
US *'Business Week'* Interview
Business Day 27 September 1985

'Accept where I am going or I will not lead you.'

As Prime Minister, NP Congress Transvaal
18 September 1979

'I am not intending to lead from behind but from in front.'

As Prime Minister, NP Congress Durban
15 August 1979

'I detest weaklings in public life. I believe in straight-forward and honest politics.'

As Prime Minister, in interview with
London *Sunday Telegraph*
18 March 1979

'People must wait and see whether I keep my promise to maintain honest and pure administration.'

As Prime Minister, SATV Interview
31 October 1978

'If I feel like I do tonight, you are likely to see a great deal more of me in the future.'

As State President, squashing rumours of
retirement, Election meeting, Stellenbosch
22 April 1987

'I believe I am what I am by the mercy of God.'

As State President, NP Congress Durban
14 August 1986

'I have come to the realisation and conviction that the struggle in South Africa is not between White, Black and Brown, but between Christian civilized standards and the powers of chaos.'

As Prime Minister, Warrenton
24 July 1982

'We must so accept each other, so respect each other, help each other in such a way to enlarge South Africa's richness in its diversity. This is our God-given duty.'

As Prime Minister, after his election
28 September 1978

'The separation of races happened long before the Nationalist Government. God separated the races.'

As Prime Minister, to an Austrian journalist
during European tour.
From *Venture into the Exterior* by John Scott
***The Star* 3 September 1984**

'Communists are misusing the Bible and liberals are misusing Christianity to sow their disorder throughout the world.'

As Prime Minister,
NP Congress Parow Cape
14 October 1981

'The God that I believe in is big enough to be the God of others as well.'

**As Prime Minister,
Springbok 15 May 1982**

'I hate no black man. I hate no brown man. The same God that made me put them there too. My God is not only for Afrikaners.'

**As Prime Minister,
NP Congress Transvaal 18 September 1979**

'We are determined to maintain peace as long as God grants us the power to control the destiny of our country.'

**As Minister of Defence, Cape Congress
of the NP Cape Town
24 August 1977**

'Don't shout at me, but pray for me. I am an ordinary man with few talents. I need the help of all.'

As Prime Minister, to a black audience in Kangwane
30 August 1979

'I'll walk with God
I'll take His Hand
And I will walk with Him into a better brighter South African future.'

On his return to Waterkloof, Pretoria,
as the new Prime Minister
30 September 1978

'Whites cannot wish the Blacks and Coloureds away. The best foundation stone for the future is the Christian message: Do unto others as you would have them do unto you.'

As Prime Minister,
NP Congress Bloemfontein
6 September 1979

'Unique arrangements need to be made for our situation.'

As Minister of Defence,
Republic Day Speech, University of Pretoria
26 May 1977

'We do not know what tomorrow will bring. We are not prophets. This is a step in the dark. We can only proceed into the future with faith.'

As Prime Minister, introducing the
4th Amendment to the Constitution Bill,
The Star 23 May 1980

'South Africa has nothing to hide.'

> **As Minister of Defence, in his offer to the
> *Guardian* newspaper to visit the operational
> area in SWA/Namibia to investigate
> allegations of torture
> 1 September 1976
> On 5 September 1976 this offer was withdrawn**

'Never in the history of this country have so few people done so much for so many without acknowledgement by the international community.'

> **As State President, referring to the ruling
> National Party House of Assembly
> 17 August 1987**

'The Afrikaner has not stolen the country from anyone.'

As Prime Minister,
House of Assembly
2 February 1982

'We [the Afrikaner] can't go back to the Netherlands, they won't take us any more. We can't go back to Germany, to Great Britain, to France.'

As State President, on South Africa being the
home of the Afrikaner
House of Delegates (Indian)
20 August 1987

'We dare not see ourselves as a chosen people. We are called people – called to a particular task, just as every nation is a called people.'

As Prime Minister, on Day of the Covenant
rally Hartenbosch
17 December 1983

'Leave alone what belongs to the Afrikaner – we have been mocked enough in the past.'

As Minister of Defence, to English Opposition press Riversdal 14 October 1972

'It is totally wrong to create the idea that we are a bad lot of Nazis denying other people their rights in South Africa.'

As State President, interview on *NBC Nightline* **by Ted Koppel** *The Star* **25 March 1985**

'Without the majority of Afrikaners, this country cannot make a success of it.'

As State President, House of Assembly 28 April 1986

'Fact is that the whites, and in particular the Afrikaner, constitutes a great part of the solution.'

**As State President, House of Assembly
13 August 1987**

'The United Nations say we are racists, the HNP that we are liberals. We can't be both. Both are lies.'

**As Prime Minister, NP Rally Pietersburg
25 August 1979**

'But if there is unfair unreasonable reaction to all the good-will shown by responsible white leaders in South Africa, I would not be surprised if my own people turned to the right, because we are not going to abdicate our position in South Africa.'

**As State President, interviewed in the
Washington Times
The Star 8 March 1986**

'There are attempts upon attempt to portray the Afrikaner as dishonest. We are not more dishonest than any other nation.'

**As Prime Minister,
NP Congress Port Elizabeth
29 September 1980**

'I am tired of constantly hearing how guilty the Afrikaner and the National Party are and the time has come that this myth be crushed.'

**As State President, at the annual conference of
the Afrikaner Studentebond Stellenbosch
15 April 1985**

'We are sick and tired of being represented as thugs. I want to warn those who continue to besmirch our public representatives that if they continue in this way they will unleash forces of which the end results cannot be foreseen.'

**As Prime Minister, in House of Assembly
re the press reportage on the
Erasmus Report and Info Scandal
7 December 1978**

'The Government will not allow itself to be blackmailed.'

**As Prime Minister, House of Assembly:
on Eschel Rhoodie's threats, while in hiding,
to expose involvement in Info Scandal
14 March 1979**

'We must learn something from the struggle of the Afrikaners. When we were a deprived people we actually became stronger because we were encouraged to strive for things we wanted.'

**As State President,
Election meeting Sasolburg
1 May 1987**

'I am not less of an Afrikaner when I meet Coloureds around a table to discuss matters of mutual interest concerning our land.'

**As Minister of Defence, at a Public Meeting
in Blanco near George
14 October 1977**

'Lord Milner had, in the forced Peace of Vereeniging [that ended the Boer War] ensured there was to be no franchise for black people after the introduction of self-government – which was never intended. It was only after half a century that an Afrikaner government started doing something about black rights.'

**As State President, unveiling monument to
Boer War victims at Delareyville
10 October 1985**

'It's a scandal that the Afrikaner should be spoken of like this in his own fatherland by people who owe him thanks. You've got apartheid on the brain. Why don't you berate the colonialists? If it weren't for the National Party you'd never have sat here. It's the closest you've got to governing in your history.'

**As State President, castigating members of
the Labour Party in the House of Representatives
19 August 1987**

'There are people in my country, and also many others, who believe in the inherent superiority of the white man, and the inferiority of the black man, but let me assure you they are not members of my government.'

As Prime Minister, in speech to the Swiss-SA Association in Switzerland during European Tour – from *Venture into the Exterior* by John Scott *The Star* 3 September 1984

'The Republic of South Africa has a new formula under the National Party's leadership: black nations can get freedom without firing shots or revolution.'

As Prime Minister, Graaff-Reinet 26 May 1984

'I intend carrying out the policy of my party with all its consequences.'

As Prime Minister, at the press conference after his election. Cape Town 28 September 1978

'We have our own system, but it must continue on Christian Principles.'

**As Prime Minister, Upington
28 July 1979**

'We have outgrown the outdated colonial system of paternalism, as well as the outdated concept of apartheid.'

**As State President, opening Parliament,
Cape Town
31 January 1986**

'Politics *per se* are not dirty, but politics are dirtied by people.'

**As Prime Minister, NP meeting Knysna
7 November 1980**

'Our enemies latched onto the word "apartheid" and in a very sly manner transformed it into the strongest weapon in the onslaught against freedom and civilization in our country.'

As State President, at the passing-out parade
SA Police College Pretoria
20 June 1986

'Undoubtedly this Afrikaans word [apartheid] was changed into a swearword in the international community, whether or not people understand anything about it.'

As State President,
NP Congress Port Elizabeth
30 September 1985

'Racial discrimination in South Africa is a heritage of the old colonial period.'

As Prime Minister, in BBC Interview
29 May 1979

'I have already repeatedly stated that if 'apartheid' means:

political domination of one group over another;

the exclusion of many communities from the political decision-making process;

injustice and inequality in the opportunities available to any community; and

racial discrimination and encroachment upon human dignity;

then the South African Government shares in the rejection of the concept'

**As State President,
NP Congress Port Elizabeth
30 September 1985**

'Those who want to seize power shout that apartheid lives. Well, those who want to share power say that it is dying. That is the reality.'

As State President, in a personalised advert in the press.
Sunday Star **2 February 1986**

'One type [of apartheid] is dead. Time has caught up with it and it is dying of starvation.'

As Prime Minister, replying to a question concerning the death of apartheid.
House of Assembly 23 April 1979

'This so-called terrible word [apartheid]: if it means oppression, if it means destroying the rights of people, then I'm not for it. If it means oppression I reject it, if it means positive development, I accept it.'

As Prime Minister, giving his victory speech at Union Buildings Pretoria after a YES vote in the Referendum.
3 November 1983

'First we are attacked because of so-called "petty apartheid". Now "grand apartheid" gets the blame. It is neither of the two. It is the peaceful co-existence of a diversity of cultures.'

As State President, NP Congress Durban
12 August 1986

'There is not an Indian community in the world which is better off than the Indians in South Africa.
That is the type of apartheid that I stand for. That is the type of apartheid which is not dead.'

As Prime Minister, House of Assembly
23 April 1979

'Leave South Africa to the South Africans and with God's help we can go forward in faith.'

As State President, *Financial Mail*
1 August 1986

'Our problems are not so much racial as radicals wish to make them.'

As Prime Minister,
in US *Business Week* **interview**
Sunday Express **4 April 1982**

'South Africa's relations with the rest of the world are going through a testing phase. This is not of recent origin.'

As State President,
opening parliament Cape Town
30 January 1987

'Unfortunately [South Africa] has been badly repaid for her loyalty because the West has expelled her from the family circle while befriending the most dictatorial regimes on Earth.'

As State President,
interview with Paris *Figaro*
The Star **8 December 1986**

'Without us the free world will lose its strength and lose the fight. With South Africa the world can end the shooting.'

**On arrival at Waterkloof airbase as
the new Prime Minister
30 September 1978**

'It must not be taken for granted that South Africa will take part in a war on the side of the West. If it suits us, we can remain neutral.'

As Minister of Defence
The Times **London
28 January 1977**

'We are prepared to negotiate with the world.'

As Minister of Defence, on SWA issue
NP Congress Bloemfontein
6 September 1978

43

'We want the world to know we are doing everything to ensure that no group or race suffer under another.'

As Minister of Defence, opening a new rifle range at the Daniel Pienaar High School, Port Elizabeth 20 May 1978

'There exists in some Western countries a lack of appreciation of the complicated situation in Southern Africa.'

As Minister of Defence, Republic Day Speech, University of Pretoria 26 May 1977

'I am not prepared to cut my own throat for the sake of world opinion.'

As Prime Minister, dealing with the dismantling of discrimination House of Assembly 7 February 1979

'It is a sick world in which South Africa has to make its way.'

As Prime Minister, NP Meeting Cape Town
8 March 1980

'It's a psychological onslaught, an economic one, a diplomatic one, a military onslaught – a total onslaught.'

As Minister of Defence,
House of Assembly
17 April 1978

'Where in the world is there a just society which can throw stones at us?'

**As Minister of Defence, at the Republic
Day celebrations in Potchefstroom
24 May 1976**

'If elements overseas that are opposed to South Africa have their way, it will lead to poverty and a bloodbath.'

**As State President, House of Assembly
20 February 1985**

'You must be very careful not to allow South Africa to be exploded.'

As State President, interviewed for
London Weekend Television **by Brian Walden**
Financial Mail
31 May 1985

'Don't push us too far . . . Don't push us too far.'

As State President, NP Congress Durban
15 August 1985

'Don't put us with our backs to the wall. You might find a far different situation if you did.'

As State President, House of Assembly
20 February 1985

'I am going to keep order in South Africa and nobody in the world is going to stop me.'

As State President, interviewed on
NBC Nightline **by Ted Koppel**
The Star **25 March 1985**

'Moenie die tier in die Afrikaner wakker maak nie. U kan te ver gaan met ons.'

**As Minister van Verdediging, Volksraad
25 Junie 1976**

['Do not awaken the tiger in the Afrikaner. You would be pushing us too far.'

**As Minister of Defence, House of Assembly
25 June 1976]**

'I take the strongest exception to your interference in affairs of which you know nothing. Had your attitude prevailed in the era of your illustrious forebears you, as an avowed liberal, would now have been under the domination of the Nazi Regime.'

**As Prime Minister, replying to a letter
from British MP Tony Benn**
Sunday Times **12 August 1984**

'I would appreciate it if Mrs Thatcher withholds herself from South African affairs.'

**As Prime Minister, on the British PM's
stating racial separation as the
cause of SA's tension.
Hartenbosch 29 September 1983**

'The fact is that the Westminster system has not worked anywhere in Africa − not even in England, because the Scots and the Welsh are moving away from it.'

**As Minister of Defence,
at the NP Congress in Port Elizabeth
20 September 1976**

'Britain's support would be of great value.'

As Prime Minister, in article in London
Sunday Express during visit to UK
3 June 1984

'I know Mrs Thatcher – I've met her and I know some
of her ministers. I don't think that they will interfere in
our affairs, because they have so many other problems
themselves to solve that they won't have time to solve our
problems for us.'

As Prime Minister, in BBC interview
29 May 1979

'Rather than embarrass the Prime Minister herself with
my admiration, it would be more diplomatic to say I got
on famously with Denis [her husband].'

As State President, interviewed by
Peregrine Worsthorne on his meeting with
Mrs Thatcher London *Sunday Telegraph*
14 April 1985

'Of course one must have a drink to wind down. Either a small white wine or a whisky. These days, whisky has become very expensive, so it's more often I take a good South African wine.'

London *Sunday Times* Magazine
29 March 1987

'I have been to Switzerland before, but not to this house [Paul Kruger's home] or to a Swiss bank.'

On European Tour aş Prime Minister,
Geneva
31 May 1984

'You have to be a dumb person not to learn from the ideas of others. But I am not prepared to build the type of wall you built in Berlin. In South Africa we only build walls for houses.'

> **As Prime Minister, to a *Voice of America* journalist in Berlin during European Tour from *Venture into the Exterior* by John Scott *The Star* 3 September 1984**

'I am not going to Moscow.'

> **As Prime Minister, at press conference in Vienna during his European Tour in answer to the question: Would you say where you are going? 8 June 1984**

'South Africa is not in a state of insurrection, just as little as is Europe.'

> **As State President, in interview with *Die Welt* *The Citizen* 20 October 1986**

'Sweep your own doorstep before you sweep ours. In the time it takes to keep you off our backs, we could have swept our own doorstep and have been well on the way to having a model state.'

**As Minister to Defence, to the American
Civil Rights Movement
NP Election meeting Kempton Park
Johannesburg 18 October 1977**

'We did not stand still at the Great Trek.'

**As Prime Minister, opening the Central
Consolidation Committee of the Plural
Relations Commission
7 June 1979**

'All we want to have is more time for South Africa.'

**As Prime Minister, NP meeting Witbank
16 September 1980**

'I know what happened in Rhodesia. I was Minister of Defence and I know that without us they wouldn't have lasted as long as they did.'

As Prime Minister, Knysna
20 October 1983

'The Rhodesian people will have to live with the decision they have taken.'

As Prime Minister, NP meeting Cape Town
8 March 1980

'The wind of change has become an African storm threatening the very survival of nations of the continent.'

As State President,
NP Congress Bloemfontein
2 September 1986

'I previously predicted the communists would run down Zaïre and Zambia and I still believe Zambia's time will come.'

Cape Times
20 March 1977

'President Kaunda does not fit into the communist camp.'

**As Minister of Defence, at a press conference in Windhoek SWA on the invasion of Zaïre.
5 April 1977**

'I know Mr Kaunda well.'

As State President, interviewed in
Figaro
15 May 1985

'Botswana would not even survive a week without us.'

As State President, in interview with
Figaro
The Star **8 December 1986**

'Let us for the sake of Africa, bury our imported quarrels and tackle our many problems together.'

As State President, to African leaders,
NP Congress Bloemfontein
2 September 1986

'Whatever the differences between our governments, I had great respect for him.'

**As State President, in his message of
condolence to Mozambique on the death
of President Samora Machel
The Star 20 October 1986**

'You cannot be responsible for something of which you have no knowledge.'

**As Prime Minister, commenting on the
Info Scandal House of Assembly
7 December 1978**

'Unless Mozambique co-operates with South Africa it has no future. It will go down the drain.'

**As State President, at a press conference
in Paris 12 November 1986**

'The Cubans are not in Africa out of love.'

**As Minister of Defence on
Cubans in Angola
Beeld 22 January 1978**

'I don't want war. War is dangerous. War is very expensive.'

**As Prime Minister,
NP Congress Parow Cape
12 October 1981**

'As long as there is a National Party Government, we won't hand over South West Africa to the authority of SWAPO.'

**As Prime Minister, in an interview in
the *New York Times*
29 April 1981**

'Everyone serving over the border in Angola is doing so on a voluntary basis.'

As Minister of Defence,
Rand Daily Mail
9 January 1976

'We went into Angola with America's knowledge and approval – and they left us in the lurch.'

As Minister of Defence,
House of Assembly
17 April 1978

'South Africa is the scapegoat for America's bad conscience.'

As State President, Election meeting
Lichtenburg
25 March 1987

'What about their [The US] bad conditions, after all their so-called human rights, in New York?'

As Minister of Defence, to the
Cape Congress of the NP
23 August 1977

'[The U.S.] was in the grips of a sickly humanism, trying to appease Africa and at the same time, feed the hungry crocodile from Moscow.'

As Prime Minister, in an interview
with London *Sunday Telegraph*
18 March 1979

'I can't understand why [the United States] co-operates with countries where freedom is destroyed by dictatorships and attack a country where we are working for freedom and liberty.'

As State President, interviewed by
the *Wall Street Journal*
***The Star* 22 October 1985**

'The United States needs a man at the helm who knows some psychology, who would know that you can't try to dictate to a people from abroad without stiffening their resistance.'

**As Minister of Defence, interviewed in the *New York Times*
28 October 1977**

'From time to time I watch television. My favourites are Wild West stories. In earlier days I used to read them.'

**London *Sunday Times* Magazine
29 March 1987**

'[Ronald Reagan] will always be remembered by South Africa for having preached good sense and tried to maintain it.'

**As State President, House of Assembly
13 August 1987**

'It is good to know that the leader of the Free World acknowledges and appreciates the strategic importance of South Africa.'

**As Prime Minister, reacting to
Ronald Reagan's positive attitude to
reformist steps in SA
The Star 4 March 1981**

'The United States of America has already declared an economic war against us for the most absurd and sanctimonious reasons.'

**As State President, on Reagan's limited
sanctions, George
21 November 1986**

'I am not going to allow foreign people to foist a minority government with guns on the majority of the people of South West Africa.'

As Prime Minister,
Press Conference Pretoria
19 October 1978

'We want the right attitudes to prevail. Apart from the negative task of shooting when necessary, there is the bigger task of winning the hearts and beliefs of the people.'

As Minister of Defence, on SWA border war
NP Congress Bloemfontein
7 September 1978

'It should be noted that refugees are crossing the border from southern Angola to South West Africa – not the other way round. There is no aggression from our side.'

As Minister of Defence, denying claims
that SA forces have been shelling
southern Angola
9 November 1976

'Although we have given the people of South West Africa the right to decide their future for themselves, we will not allow the barrel of the gun to decide what "red flag" will fly in Windhoek.'

**As Prime Minister, Nylstroom
18 November 1982**

'If we allow the communist flag over Windhoek, South Africa's enemies will stand with their rifles on the banks of the Orange River.'

**As State President,
Election meeting Lichtenburg
25 March 1987**

'We stand by the wishes of the people of South West Africa.'

**As Prime Minister, in reply to UN
proposals for a ceasefire
House of Assembly
5 March 1979**

'No more mine-laying. No more murder. No more abduction of women and children. No more attacks on headmen. No more raids across the border. So long as these conditions do not exist, there will be no withdrawal [from SWA] of South African troops.'

**As Prime Minister, House of Assembly
8 March 1979**

'The Russians make no secret of their desire of the control of South Africa, which holds the key to the control of the seaways of the Atlantic.'

**As Minister of Defence, opening a new
rifle range at the Daniel Pienaar
High School Port Elizabeth
20 May 1978**

'I'm an African.'

As Prime Minister, interviewed in the
New York Times
The Star **17 February 1983**

'I know African leaders listen to me, even if they do not admit it.'

**As State President,
NP Congress Bloemfontein
2 September 1986**

'If it is an embarrassment to those countries, I keep quiet, go there, do my job and come back.'

As Prime Minister, on his secret visits abroad. *Leadership SA* **interview**
Sunday Times **16 October 1983**

'I even received a decoration from one of them.'

**As Minister of Defence, commenting on his secret missions to African states. House of Assembly
11 September 1974**

'I will go [to black townships] if I'm asked. I will go anywhere where I am welcome.'

As Prime Minister, Seshego, Lebowa, after addressing Lebowa Legislative Assembly 10 August 1979

'We do not have in South Africa a white nation and a black nation, we have different nations.'

As Prime Minister, in US *Business Week* interview *Sunday Express* 4 April 1982

'Our different indigenous peoples, White, Black and Brown have never been, and do not intend being, slaves now or in the future.'

As Prime Minister, Press Conference Pretoria 19 October 1978

'We have a country of different minorities – a white minority and black minorities.'

As State President, interviewed on
London Weekend Television by Brian Walden
Financial Mail 31 May 1985

'Partition [of South Africa] is not practically possible. It is a dream.'

As State President,
Election meeting Sasolburg
1 May 1987

'We believe that a Confederation of States is in the best interests of Southern Africa.'

As Prime Minister, opening the
Gazankulu Legislative Assembly in Giyani
12 March 1982

'Each member state [in the proposed constellation of Southern African States] will be sovereign and independent and one will not be able to make laws or decisions for another.'

As Prime Minister, *Die Burger*
18 March 1980

'If a state such as Luxembourg can be independent, why can black urban communities (i.e. Soweto) close to our metropolitan areas (i.e. Johannesburg) not receive autonomy as City-States?'

As State President, NP Congress Durban
Financial Mail
15 August 1986

'There is not one single black man in this country who is not linked to a black homeland.'

As Prime Minister,
NP Congress Bloemfontein
4 September 1980

'We cannot give away the whole of South Africa merely to create economically viable black states.'

As Prime Minister,
NP Congress Bloemfontein
4 September 1980

'Let me tell you that 50% of South Africa's culturable land consists of black national states.'

As State President, interviewed on
***NBC Nightline* by Ted Koppel**
on arid homelands
***The Star* 25 March 1985**

'You can go and interview a black defence minister now. You can just go to Transkei.'

As State President, interviewed by the
***Wall Street Journal* on question if a**
black could one day become of defence minister
***The Star* 22 October 1985**

'I may know where I want to go, but not how to get there.'

**As Prime Minister, opening the
Gazankulu Legislative Assembly in Giyani
12 March 1982**

'I believe that we are today crossing the Rubicon. There can be no turning back.'

As State President, NP Congress Durban
15 August 1985

'What do we get? [After fighting in two world wars, Korea and taking part in the Berlin airlift.] A weapons boycott and preparations for sanctions.'

As Minister of Defence,
NP meeting Piketberg Cape
4 March 1978

'I really hope the Western powers aren't going to use sanctions against us – they might find that this is only one side of the coin!'

As Prime Minister, in a BBC Interview
29 May 1979

'If sanctions are applied it will be a question of cutting off your nose to spite your face.'

As Prime Minister,
Press Conference Pretoria
19 October 1978

'If selected sanctions in one or other form are applied against us, we shall fight them tooth and nail.'

As Prime Minister, to foreign
correspondents in Pretoria
18 November 1980

'Sanctions, boycotts and embargoes have never worked anywhere.'

As State President
The Citizen
28 April 1987

'Sanctions will weaken the poor and hamper the process of reform. This will encourage violence and revolutionary change.'

As State President, opening the 3rd World Congress of Brahman Breeders Johannesburg 24 March 1986

'South Africans will not allow themselves to be humiliated in order to prevent sanctions. We do not desire it and we do not seek it, but if we are forced to go it alone, then so be it.'

As State President, House of Assembly 12 June 1986

'The only way to apply a proper policy of sanctions would be to form a blockade around our coasts.'

As Minister of Defence, speaking at his election office in his constituency of George 28 October 1977

'I have instructed that the South African institutions concerned urgently make a further survey of the numbers of foreign workers, as well as where they work, so that government can consider effective action to repatriate them [in case of sanctions against South Africa].'

As State President, Potchefstroom 29 July 1985

'Not only will we survive [sanctions] we will emerge stronger on the other side.'

As State President, NP Congress Durban
Financial Mail
15 August 1986

'Let me say no attempt to overthrow our country by embargoes, subversion or revolution will succeed. Our security forces are trained to withstand revolution.'

**As Minister of Defence, to the
Cape Congress of the NP
23 August 1977**

'Do not think that South Africa cannot have a revolution. Revolution is not a remote possibility.'

**As Prime Minister,
NP meeting Koedoespoort
27 August 1979**

'If somebody does try violence in South Africa, he will laugh on the other side of his face.'

**As Prime Minister,
Referendum meeting George
26 September 1983**

'South Africa must stand united against the spirit of revolution incited against the country from abroad.'

As State President,
opening Parliament Cape Town
30 January 1987

'The point of view that a paradise on Earth can be achieved by violent revolution, is nothing but a dangerous and totally naïve dream.'

As State President,
opening Parliament Cape Town
30 January 1987

'We cannot talk to leaders who are trying to create revolution in South Africa.'

As Prime Minister, commenting on suggested
meetings with ANC and SWAPO
Cape Town 4 April 1983

'We cannot allow forces of evil [the ANC] to commit murder and wanton destruction in this country.'

As State President,
at award ceremony Cape Town Castle
16 February 1985

'South Africa has the will and the capacity to break the ANC.'

As State President, House of Delegates
21 May 1986

'I want to warn young people who lend their ears to radicals and who play around with the music from Lusaka – they will end up inside the bear's fur coat, but they will no longer be able to live.'

As State President,
Election meeting Pietermaritzburg
30 April 1987

'The ANC is laughing up their sleeves at the naïvety of useful idiots who, as Lenin puts it, can be used to further the aims of the first phase of the Revolution.'

**As State President, on the
'Dakar Safari' to talk to ANC
House of Assembly 13 August 1987**

'The longer clumsy politicians and rash victims woo the ANC, the longer it will take to get the ANC, as an accountable and responsible party, to join other South African interested parties around the negotiating table.'

**As State President, in parliament on
'Dakar Safari'**
The Star **15 August 1987**

'I regard [discussions with the ANC] as unwise and even disloyal to the young men who are sacrificing their lives in defending South Africa's safety.'

**As State President, on businessmen
meeting the ANC in Lusaka**
The Citizen **8 September 1985**

'I do not see why I should have to talk to terrorists, when it is not expected of Britain, France or Germany to talk to terrorists.'

As State President,
Election meeting Stellenbosch
22 April 1987

'Who can expect me to hold discussions with the ANC and then look a black or white parent of a child who died in ANC violence in the eye?'

As State President,
NP Congress Pretoria
20 September 1985

'[The ANC] knows it is not supported by the majority in South Africa.'

As State President, interviewed by
Die Welt
***The Citizen* 20 October 1986**

'We will not talk to these people, [the ANC] we will fight them.'

**As State President,
House of Assembly
10 June 1987**

'If [the leaders of the ANC] relinquish violence and stop living in luxury outside the country's borders at the expense of foreign governments and come back to their own country to take part in a constitutional process, of course they can share in constitutional processes.'

**As State President, in Parliament
The Star
15 August 1987**

'I don't care what a man's politics are – as long as he is not a Communist.'

**As Minister of Defence, Queenstown
22 November 1969**

'I can put it plainly that the Government has never said that all ANC members are communists.'

**As State President,
House of Assembly
17 April 1986**

'We think [Marxism] is a hollow cry. We think our system is better.'

**As Prime Minister, visiting Taiwan
Taipei 17 October 1980**

'The freedom of one person so easily becomes the oppression of another.'

As State President,
NP Congress Durban
12 August 1986

'If we let [Nelson Mandela] free, we will set free an arch-Marxist supported by Marxists from Moscow.'

**As Prime Minister,
NP meeting Stellenbosch
10 April 1980**

'Mandela has overstepped the mark. He has broken the law. The judiciary of this country has put him where he belongs according to the rules of democracy.'

**As Prime Minister,
NP meeting Stellenbosch
10 April 1980**

'South Africa is a democratically-governed state and it is a civilized state; and I am not going to liberate people from jail who are not prepared to tell me beforehand that they won't take up arms against the State.'

**As State President, in interview with
ARD German TV
Financial Mail transcript 5 September 1986**

'Knowing [Mandela] will start up with violence again, I, as a responsible head of state, must release him so he can carry on with his violence, and then arrest him? What a nonsensical argument.'

**As State President,
in the House of Delegates
23 April 1986**

'He [Mandela] is keeping himself in jail. The moment he renounces violence, he will be set free.'

**As State President,
House of Assembly
28 April 1986**

'[Mandela] is not prepared to reject violence. I am not as Head of State going to see him in jail to enquire from him whether he is prepared to talk to me.'

**As State President,
BBC Radio interview
17 April 1987**

'Mr Mandela is therefore in effect being jailed by the South African Communist Party and its affiliate the African National Congress.'

**As State President, on Mandela not
renouncing violence as a condition
for freedom
Opening of Parliament
31 January 1986**

'It is therefore not the South African Government which now stands in the way of Mr Mandela's freedom. It is himself. The choice is his.'

**As State President, after offering Mandela
freedom if he renounces violence
House of Assembly
31 January 1985**

'If I were to release Mr Nelson Mandela on humanitarian grounds, could Captain Wynand du Toit, Andrei Sakharov and Anatoly Shcharansky not also be released on humanitarian grounds?'

**As State President,
opening Parliament Cape Town
31 January 1986**

'Nelson Mandela can rot in prison until he dies or I die, whichever takes longer.'

**As supposedly said by him at a meeting
for foreign correspondents in Cape Town
and later used in an opposition election
advert but denied and an apology demanded
February 1987**

'It was a tasteless attempt to belittle not only my person, but the image of South Africa.'

**As State President, referring to the Opposition
use of his rumoured 'Mandela can rot'
comment. Election meeting Johannesburg
4 May 1987**

'I can also enjoy a joke from time to time.'

**As Prime Minister, opening the SA
Agricultural Union Congress Durban
20 October 1981**

'South Africa is not a push-over.'

As State President, interviewed on
***NBC Nightline* by Ted Koppel**
***The Star* 25 March 1985**

'We have a laager with open doors.'

As State President, in interview with
***ARD* German TV**
***Financial Mail* transcript 5 September 1986**

'Nobody should ever expect us to confuse reform with surrender.'

As State President,
NP Congress Pretoria
19 September 1986

'We will not go to the moon.'

**As State President,
NP Congress Durban
14 August 1986**

'We will fight to the last drop of blood to maintain an orderly country.'

**Election meeting Stellenbosch
22 November 1977**

'I don't want to sound trigger-happy but South Africa's honour is at stake.'

**As Minister of Defence, promising that
no soldier would leave SWA as long
as SWAPO terrorised the area.
NP Congress Natal 16 August 1978**

'If South Africa wants to defend itself and protect its borders, South Africa must pay a price it has not yet paid.'

As Minister of Defence,
at the NP Congress Bloemfontein
9 September 1977

'We will get hurt, but we will not be the only ones to get hurt.'

As Minister of Defence, on war in South Africa
Public meeting Calvinia Cape
21 March 1977

'You won't force South Africans to commit national suicide.'

As State President, meeting Sir Geoffrey Howe
Financial Mail
1 August 1986

'It is possible that more lives will be placed on the altar of South African patriotism and freedom in the future.'

**As Minister of Defence,
on the presentation of *Honoris Crux* Medals,
Voortrekkerhoogte
27 November 1976**

'If we are forced to bow to a conventional war against us, we shall fight a guerilla war. We shall never surrender.'

**As Minister of Defence,
interviewed in the *New York Times*
28 October 1977**

'South Africa has no territorial demands. She does not want to follow a policy of aggression against anyone.'

**As Minister of Defence,
at the NP Congress Windhoek SWA
on eve of UN deadline for the
withdrawal from SWA of SA
25 August 1976**

'Any country that gives shelter to terrorists will have to deal with our security forces.'

**As Prime Minister,
House of Assembly
1 February 1983**

'We will not take part in any operations in neighbouring countries without Parliament first taking a decision on it.'

**As Minister of Defence
The Times London
28 January 1977**

'We have only delivered the first instalment and if necessary we'll strike again.'

'I now want to state unequivocally, clearly and pertinently to the world and the Angolan Regime that South Africa has no intention of attacking Angola.'

'We are there to keep intruders on the other side of the border. We are doing so, and we are doing it well. They sometimes cross to plunder, but then they immediately run for the border again.'

'The South African Defence Force was not, and never will be, busy with the training of terrorists or people with the purpose of overthrowing another government.'

**As Minister of Defence, reacting
to an *Observer* newspaper report
that SA was training guerillas
to overthrow the Zambian Government
5 June 1976**

'No responsible official gave his approval to the abortive coup [of the Seychelles by a group of white mercenaries from SA].'

**As Prime Minister,
House of Assembly
1 February 1983**

'We are not looking for a war.'

**As Minister of Defence,
House of Assembly
5 May 1969**

'Violence and revolution have never served anybody. I pledge myself to prevent violence. I and my Government will strive for a non-violent South Africa.'

As Prime Minister, NP meeting Cape Town
8 March 1980

'Let the world know this. They may boycott us, but we will manufacture more and more of our own weapons. We will make them with the help of the Coloureds and Blacks. They are already assisting us and I am proud of their contribution.'

As Minister of Defence,
at an Election meeting in his own
constituency of George in the Cape.
17 October 1977

'Confrontation is not my choice, but the State will maintain stability and order with all the power at its disposal.'

As Prime Minister, on SABC
14 March 1982

'If violence is used as a final instrument something will happen in South Africa that the proponents of violence cannot even dream of.'

As Prime Minister,
House of Assembly
2 February 1982

'The South African security forces will leave no stone unturned in their endeavours to defend our country and its people.'

As State President,
opening Parliament Cape Town
30 January 1987

'The State has not yet used its full might during the outbreaks of violence. If it does people will be hurt very much more.'

As Prime Minister, on SATV
22 June 1980

'If they want confrontation and bloodshed despite my efforts, then I say to them let it come, the sooner the better.'

**As Prime Minister,
House of Assembly
1 February 1983**

'We are being painted into a corner in a well-orchestrated propaganda campaign.'

**As State President,
to Foreign Correspondents Association
Johannesburg
31 October 1985**

'People must not take the law into their own hands. It is the State's duty to maintain law and order.'

**As Minister of Defence, commenting
on the rise of vigilante activity
in SA, to the NP Congress in
Port Elizabeth
20 September 1976**

'One match in the hands of a fool is enough to set this country alight.'

**As Prime Minister,
NP Congress Bloemfontein
30 July 1982**

'As a matter of fact I think that the chance of a civil war is becoming less and less.'

**As State President, in interview
with *ARD* German TV
Financial Mail transcript 5 September 1986**

'The Army is merely a reflection of the people themselves.'

**As Minister of Defence,
at the NP Congress Bloemfontein
9 September 1977**

'The Defence Force is not perfect, the Police are not perfect, but it is the duty of every South African to stand by the security forces to keep the country safe.'

**As Prime Minister, Parys
1 November 1982**

'This Government has not refused to shoot. It has done so. But it does so with judgement − so it can shoot again.'

**As Prime Minister,
NP Congress Pretoria
4 November 1981**

'[The use of the Defence Force in maintaining law and order] had been done in 1914, in March 1922 for the Johannesburg miners strike and in 1960 for the Sharpeville and Langa unrest.'

**As State President, Vredendal
17 November 1984**

'This isn't the first time the Government has used troops. It's a tradition in South Africa.'

**As State President, in an interview
with the *Wall Street Journal*
The Star 22 October 1985**

'Wherever the police went into action, they did so to protect people. Some instigators of violence clashed with police, so the police had to react. So I would not say the police are responsible [for violence].'

**As State President,
interviewed in *Il Giornale*
Business Day 26 June 1986**

'I deny that police shoot people without reason.'

As State President, in interview with
***ARD* German TV**
***Financial Mail* transcript 5 September 1986**

'Reference is often made to so-called "political prisoners" in South Africa with regard to persons who are serving prison sentences or detained in terms of the laws of the country.'

As State President,
NP Congress Durban
12 August 1986

'We don't put people in prison in South Africa because they differ politically from the government.'

As Prime Minister, to an Austrian
journalist during European Tour
from *Venture into the Exterior*
by John Scott
***The Star* 3 September 1984**

'We don't shoot people who are in opposition to the Government.'

Referring to police action resulting
in black deaths in Uitenhage
As State President, interviewed
on *NBC Nightline* by Ted Koppel
The Star 25 March 1985

'If there were an emergency in South Africa tomorrow, I could not say what the civilian population would do in its defence.'

**As Minister of Defence,
Cape Town Castle
8 December 1967**

'You don't go to a funeral to throw stones. I thought you went to weep.'

**As State President, interviewed on
NBC Nightline by Ted Koppel
The Star 25 March 1985**

'I do not question the existence of some grievances – whether real or imaginary – but I doubt that they gave rise to spontaneous demonstrations or were at the root of the disturbances.'

**As Minister of Defence, at the Civil
Defence Conference Pretoria on Black and
Coloured riots in the townships during 1976
3 November 1976**

'The ordinary laws of the Republic are still inadequate to bear up against this threat. I have as a result decided to proclaim again a state of emergency for the whole of the Republic, including the self-governing states.'

As State President, House of Assembly
10 June 1987

'The only thing that moves slowly these days is a funeral procession.'

As Prime Minister, on being asked
if he was moving too fast on reform
NP Congress Cape Town
26 September 1979

'The correctness of imposing a nationwide state of emergency has been substantiated by the decline in the occurrence of incidents of unrest since the middle of last year. The revolutionary climate, however, necessitates the continued maintenance of these measures of control.'

As State President,
opening Parliament Cape Town
30 January 1987

'Our security forces have over the past 24 hours been compelled to conduct certain preventative security measures.'

As State President, SATV
12 December 1986

'Not only blacks are arrested under the state of emergency. There are arrests that have been made of all population groups.'

As State President, in interview with
***ARD* German TV**
***Financial Mail* transcript 5 September 1986**

'We have a Bureau for Information and if the Press is prepared to co-operate properly with the authorities, they can get all the information which is necessary to publish.'

As State President, in interview with
***ARD* German TV**
***Financial Mail* transcript 5 September 1986**

'If the media do not want to give us the chance to do what we think must be done in South Africa, they must not blame us if we fight back. But if they think that the Government will lie down, my answer is! "Never".'

**As Prime Minister,
Sasolburg NP Meeting
8 November 1978**

'The SABC and every other member of the South African media must make a decision in these days and show where they stand.'

**As State President, at the SABC 50th
Anniversary Celebrations Johannesburg
2 August 1986**

'The entire matter concerning alternative media and alternative news agencies will have to be investigated and dealt with.'

**As State President,
House of Assembly
17 August 1987**

'The fact that the media say that there is no freedom of speech in this country in itself proves that there is freedom of speech in South Africa.'

**As Prime Minister, at Southern Cross
Fund Banquet Johannesburg
3 October 1979**

'An irresponsible Press is the greatest enemy of democracy.'

**As Prime Minister, in an interview with
London *Sunday Telegraph*
18 March 1979**

'There is too much gossiping in South Africa.'

**As Prime Minister, Warrenton
24 July 1982**

'Rumour-mongers in our midst are as great a danger to South Africa as the terrorists.'

**As Minister of Defence,
Sunday Express
30 November 1975**

'I do not want to accuse the entire opposition press, but there are elements in South Africa who are doing the work of the Russians.'

**As Prime Minister,
Brakpan
31 March 1981**

'This is why we put a stop to *The World*.'

**As Minister of Defence, at Election
Meeting in East London, after reading
from a cutting from the recently-banned
The World criticising
government policy. 11 November 1977**

'I believe in a free Press and in free news media, but I believe the best form of freedom is self-controlled responsible action.'

**As Prime Minister, on SATV
22 June 1980**

'Why do you always try and look out for a few nasty incidents?'

**As State President, to the press at
his election meeting Johannesburg
4 May 1987**

'All I want to say to you is to watch what you publish, because I am lying in watch for you.'

**As Minister of Defence, to a senior
reporter from the *Sunday Times* after
reports of a scuffle at an election
meetingn in Knysna
Sunday Times 27 November 1977**

'I enjoyed your company. I'm pleased to have got to know you better.'

**As Prime Minister, to reporters on the
Boeing having accompanied him on
his European Tour
The Star 16 June 1984**

'I was instrumental in stopping legislation which would have hampered the freedom of the Press. I asked that the Press be given a chance to put its house in order.'

**As Prime Minister,
NP Meeting Sasolburg
8 November 1978**

'I do not believe the Press should be muzzled.'

**As Minister of Defence,
NP Congress East London
The Star 3 September 1975**

'It is better to listen to what people say than to read what people write.'

**London *Sunday Times* Magazine
29 March 1987**

'Freedom without responsibility is not freedom. It is licence.'

**As Prime Minister,
House of Assembly
2 February 1982**

'I am a democrat.'

**As State President,
Election meeting Stellenbosch
22 April 1987**

'What can be more democratic than to hold elections in which people can decide for themselves who their real leaders are?'

**As Prime Minister,
Press conference Pretoria
19 October 1978**

'That is why I led the fight against [the Ossewabrandwag]. I wonder if I did not do much more [for democracy] than many others.'

As Prime Minister, on European Tour
from *Venture into the Exterior*
by John Scott
The Star **3 September 1984**

'I believe the basis of democracy is local government.'

As State President, interviewed on
London Weekend Television
by Brian Walden
Financial Mail **31 May 1985**

'What you have before you today is the best there is. It may not be perfect, but it is the best possible.'

As Prime Minister,
Kimberley Technical High School
26 October 1983

'We in South Africa prefer the danger connected with freedom under a democratic system to the safety connected with loss of freedom under a dictatorship.'

As Minister of Defence,
Pretoria University
29 July 1969

'Let us say to the black man: you have rights and we recognise those rights. Let us say the same thing to coloured people. But let us also say to them: recognise our rights. There are our aims, here is our vision and our survival plan. Let us do our duty and leave the rest to God.'

As Minister of Defence,
NP Congress East London
21 August 1978

'There is no need to liberate South Africa. We are busy with the process of liberation.'

As Prime Minister, to foreign correspondents
in Pretoria
18 November 1980

'I am prepared to grant the other man his rights on the same level as I have rights.'

As State President,
BBC Radio Interview
17 April 1987

'I am not prepared to sacrifice my rights so that the other man can dominate me with his greater numbers.'

**As State President,
BBC Radio interview
17 April 1987**

'While my people were oppressed as a minority group, we fought for our rights.'

**As Prime Minister,
NP Meeting Knysna
7 November 1980**

'The protection [of rights] will be given on a non-racial basis . . . so much for those who still accuse us of racism.'

**As State President,
House of Assembly
17 August 1987**

'But we cannot allow ourselves to be forced to keep the policy for ever the same. There is a difference between policy and principles.'

As Prime Minister, Upington
28 July 1979

'I have said in public no law is a holy cow. Old Israel choked on a number of its laws. I am not prepared to let this country choke on laws.'

As Prime Minister,
House of Assembly
20 April 1983

'Unless we can succeed in bridging the gap between the First World way of life and activity in South Africa and the Third World way of life, political reform will serve no purpose.'

**As State President,
House of Delegates
20 August 1987**

'We cannot travel the whole reform road in our time.'

**As State President,
NP Congress Pretoria
20 September 1985**

'The more we reform the more we are condemned.'

**As State President, to Foreign
Correspondents Association Johannesburg
31 October 1985**

'People must get their perspectives right. If a respectable black man rides in an aeroplane he needs a place to sleep.'

**As Prime Minister,
NP Congress Bloemfontein
4 September 1980**

'I am in favour of the removal of hurtful unnecessary discriminatory measures. Many of these have already been removed, but I am not in favour of a system of forced integration and not in favour of endangering the right of self-determination of my own people.'

**As Prime Minister,
NP Congress Durban
15 August 1979**

'I will continuously endeavour to create peace between whites and coloureds without creating an integrated society.'

**As Prime Minister,
House of Assembly
2 February 1982**

'As long as I live reform will continue only on the basis of protection for the white man.'

**As State President,
Election meeting Pietermaritzburg
30 April 1987**

'I don't apologise that I stand for separate residential areas.'

**As Prime Minister,
NP Congress Durban
20 August 1982**

'The rich people buy their apartheid with large residences and properties. The poor man must live wherever he can afford. I'm on the side of the white worker.'

**As State President,
Election meeting Ermelo
28 February 1987**

'Our residential areas are of the utmost importance, particularly in big cities, for the protection of poor white workers.'

**As State President,
Election meeting Ermelo
28 February 1987**

'The Group Areas Act has nothing to do with the free enterprise system. It is a social measure guaranteeing the right of different population groups to acquire property and have it registered in their own names.'

**As Prime Minister, briefing the Press
Pretoria
12 January 1981**

'I say make [the Group Areas Act] more flexible so that it can be applied with understanding.'

**As State President,
NP Congress Durban
14 August 1986**

'[The Group Areas Act] can be changed. I believe in the Christian approach. But at the same time I never read in the Bible that to be a good Christian means I must commit suicide to please the other man.'

**As State President,
BBC Radio interview
17 April 1987**

'Now it is being said that the [Group Areas] Act is being infringed. Any Act is infringed at one time or another. If one man kills another, we do not abolish the law that prohibits murder. What nonsense is that?'

**As State President, in Parliament
The Star 25 March 1987**

'But [nobody] will say to me it [the Group Areas Act] worked 100 percent.'

**As State President,
House of Delegates
20 August 1987**

'If there are certain matters to be amended, and if the Group Areas Act is drastically amended, with the retention of the principles I have mentioned [the protection of group rights], then I say we can perhaps find a new solution.'

**As State President,
House of Delegates
20 August 1987**

'New solutions for new problems will be found.'

**As Minister of Defence, to the Cape
Congress of the NP Cape Town
24 August 1977**

'We must adapt or we will die.'

**As Prime Minister, in interview
with *Die Transvaler*
7 August 1979**

'There are higher things in life than to stare the whole day at the colour of another man's skin.'

As Prime Minister,
NP Congress Pretoria
18 September 1979

'The survival of the Afrikaner is not dependent on the [Immorality] Act.'

As Prime Minister,
NP meeting Cape Town
8 March 1980

'After all Moses had a mixed marriage.'

As Prime Minister,
NP Congress Bloemfontein
4 September 1980

'I don't think [the Mixed Marriages Act] is so much a protection of the white man, but I think it is a protection of coloured women.'

As Prime Minister,
in BBC interview
29 May 1979

'On the question of influx control – I can only say that the present system is outdated and too costly.'

As State President,
NP Congress Durban
15 August 1985

'We must have controls. You cannot allow every man just to go and squat where he wants to squat.'

As State President, interviewed in US
Business Week on his plans
to abolish whole system of influx control
Business Day
27 September 1985

'We do not force people [in South Africa] to move to new homes, we coerce them.'

As Prime Minister, at press conference
in Berne Switzerland – (it seems he
meant to say 'convince').
The Star 2 June 1984

'The Act on separate amenities has never worked.'

**As State President,
House of Delegates
20 August 1987**

'We have lived in this country for more than 300 years and until recently we did not have separate facilities. How did we manage without them? How illogical can we be?'

**As Prime Minister,
at NP Congress Pretoria
18 September 1979**

'We have no reason as a White nation to have a guilty conscience about our past. We are no angels — because angels on earth are few and far between, but we did not kill our indigenous population groups with liquor or destroy them with the gun after attaining our freedom. We started uplifting them and leading them to theirs.'

**As Minister of Defence, Republic Day
Speech at the University of Pretoria
26 May 1977**

'The Whites brought peace to a country where the knob-kerrie and the assegaai ruled.'

As Minister of Community Development,
Kimberley
1 March 1965

'If you drop the white man and destroy white civilization, then this country will move back to the bush.'

As Prime Minister,
NP meeting Cape Town
8 March 1980

'We know we are imperfect human beings. But we also know we live in a world of double standards.'

**As Minister of Defence,
Jan van Riebeeck Day Celebrations
Cape Town
6 April 1978**

'South Africans who are born and bred to serve this country will stay here because they know that we will survive.'

**As Minister of Defence, on people
leaving South Africa
SATV interview 13 November 1977**

'I cannot see to the year 2030, but if I know my people, they will fight for their rights in South Africa.'

**Answering the question at an NP election
meeting in Nigel, Transvaal, if by the
year 2000 whites would be under a
Coloured and Indian majority.
5 October 1977**

'People have been predicting black majority government within five or ten years for the last 300 years.'

**As State President, Springs
24 October 1985**

'South Africa will do a lot to create good faith among all its nations, but we will never accept black majority rule.'

**As Minister of Defence,
NP Congress East London
21 August 1978**

'A National Party Government under me will not think of a unitary state with one man one vote. We reject it because it will lead to confrontation and a power struggle leading to Black dictatorship.'

**As Prime Minister,
NP Congress Cape Town
8 March 1980**

'We are not threatened by a black majority in our own border. We have a relaxed situation in Southern Africa, more relaxed conditions than in many European countries.'

**As Prime Minister,
interviewed in *Der Spiegel*
3 September 1979**

'I don't foresee that in the Westminster sense there can be eventually a black majority government because the Westminster system didn't work in Africa.'

**As State President,
BBC Radio interview
17 April 1987**

'Majority rule cannot be applied in South Africa, because we are a country with many different structures.'

**As State President,
in interview with *Die Welt*
The Citizen 20 October 1986**

'History shows that a unitary state has not been practical politics in South Africa for 300 years and will not be in the future. A unique solution will have to be found..'

**As Prime Minister, opening the Central
Consolidation Committee of the
Plural Relations Commission
7 June 1979**

'One man, one vote in a single structure in South Africa will not work. And I say the majority of responsible black people agree with me.'

**As State President, Vryburg
28 October 1985**

'I know for a fact that most leaders in their own right in South Africa and reasonable South Africans will not accept the principle of one man, one vote in a unitary system. That would lead to domination of one over the others and it would lead to chaos.'

**As State President,
NP Congress Durban
15 August 1985**

'Where in Africa is there an example of human dignity in a state which is unitary and has one man, one vote?'

**As Minister of Defence,
House of Assembly: Censure Debate
1 February 1978**

'One man, one vote will not work in South Africa, but the principle of one man, one vote can be applied in a different way and in different structures.'

**As State President,
interviewed by US *Business Week*
Business Day 27 September 1985**

'The principle of one man, one vote has long been accepted in South Africa. It all depends in which structures you want to apply it.'

'They [the various population groups in S.A. who can become completely independent in their homelands] all have one man, one vote, except for Mr Buthulezi's Zulus, because he has not yet established it by democratic procedures. This is because he has not yet held an election, but then he is a Prog pal.'

As Minister of Defence,
Election meeting Stellenbosch
22 November 1977

'[Buthulezi] is a product of policies made possible by this Government.'

As Prime Minister, Pretoria
3 November 1983

'Inkatha is its own type of Broederbond for the Zulu People.'

As Prime Minister, Pretoria
3 November 1983

'We are prepared to have majority government but on a basis of differentiation.'

As State President,
Election meeting Pietermaritzburg
30 April 1987

'We believe in the principle of one person, one vote as long as it is not in a unitary state.'

As State President, interviewed on
***London Weekend Television* by**
Brian Walden
***Financial Mail* 31 May 1985**

'One man, one vote in a system where minority rights are protected is the way to go.'

As State President, interviewed in
the *Washington Times*
***The Star* 8 March 1986**

'You can trust us.'

**As Minister of Defence,
to the Cape Congress of the NP Cape Town
24 August 1977**

'I have the co-operation of most black South Africans.'

As State President, interviewed on
NBC Nightline **by Ted Koppel**
The Star **25 March 1985**

'I have hundreds [of black leaders] that negotiate with me and Mr Heunis day after day.'

As State President,
Election meeting Stellenbosch
22 April 1987

'I receive tens of thousands of letters of support from all over the world.'

As State President, to South African
journalists in Paris, France during
an unwelcome visit to
Delville Wood Memorial
12 November 1986

'Today millions of Blacks are supporting this Government on every measure it took.'

As State President,
Election meeting Johannesburg
4 May 1987

'Wherever I go there is a spirit of goodwill.'

As State President, referring to his visits
to the black homelands and townships
House of Assembly 17 August 1987

'Gatherings [during a tour of the homelands] were opened with readings from the Scriptures and prayers, and Black people in their singing asked for the Lord's blessing to be bestowed on me. Must I say to these well-disposed Black people! "No, go away you bunch of kaffirs. I don't want to have anything to do with you"?'

As Prime Minister
at NP Congress Pretoria
18 September 1979

'Today Soweto has opened its heart to the Government of South Africa.'

**As Prime Minister, to a crowd of 5000
blacks on his visit to Soweto
31 August 1979**

'You have arranged a lovely day for us.'

**As Prime Minister, to Chairman of the
Soweto Council on arrival in Soweto
for visit
31 August 1979**

'The people are relaxed. They are friendly and there is a positive attitude among them.'

**As Prime Minister, after addressing
the Lebowa Legislative Assembly
10 August 1979**

'I greet every black man who greets me.'

As Minister of Defence,
NP meeting Hercules, Pretoria
5 April 1976

'They are people and are entitled to humane treatment.'

As Prime Minister, on urban blacks
NP meeting Oudtshoorn
17 April 1982

'Our black people are free in South Africa. They have never been slaves like the black people in America.'

As Prime Minister,
interviewed in *Time*
3 December 1979

'Over a million [blacks] come to this terrible South Africa, this Nazi regime where the jackbooting takes place and where there is not freedom.'

**As Minister of Defence, Grahamstown
20 October 1969**

'We are prepared to grant the right to blacks to live in their own communities.'

**As Prime Minister,
interviewed in *Time*
3 December 1979**

'Blacks have their own political institutions.'

**As Minister of Defence,
University of Port Elizabeth
19 August 1978**

'We cannot wish away Blacks any more than they wish us away. We are here.'

**As Prime Minister, Upington
28 July 1979**

'I cannot visualise a situation in my lifetime where we won't have black-skinned people in the Republic of South Africa.'

**As Prime Minister, reacting to
Dr Connie Mulder's claim that
one day there would be no
blacks in SA
The Star 15 April 1981**

'If we want to create [a fourth parliamentary chamber for blacks] then we have to accommodate 6 or 7 nations in it and that is absurd.'

**As State President,
House of Assembly
4 February 1987**

'If it took the United States of America generations to complete its consitution and Switzerland 400 years to complete its constitution, why must we overnight have a constitution that satisfies the world?'

As State President,
Election meeting Johannesburg
4 May 1987

'It will probably be the first time ever that a referendum is called to bring about a dictatorship.'

As Prime Minister, Port Elizabeth
15 October 1983

'When we all say the same, they say we have a dictatorship.'

As Minister of Defence, at NP meeting
in Boshoff referring to Press exploitation
of so-called party differences in the
NP that would lead to a supposed split.
10 September 1977

'I love to get in touch with the ordinary people of South Africa. It's the only way to stay human.'

London *Sunday Times* Magazine
29 March 1987

'A man cannot be a dictator if he is elected every 5 years and if his life in public is bound to the life of parliament.'

**As Prime Minister, answering question
if the State President would have
dictorial powers
Press Conference in Pretoria
The Star 16 September 1983**

'I am not prepared to deviate from the Constitution.'

**As State President, asked about changes
in the Group Areas Act
House of Assembly 23 April 1985**

'In the present constitution the relevant clause [of a maximum 5 year term for Parliament] is even entrenched. The government has no intention whatsoever of deviating from this principle. Consequently an amendment will be tabled during the present session with a view to determining the maximum term of each House separately to be 5 years.'

**As State President, House of Assembly
13 August 1987**

'Call me Pee Vee as you have always done in the past, because that is the sign that we still have contact with each other.'

On his homecoming as Prime Minister, George
8 October 1978

'I don't know why people take life so seriously – after all you'll never get out alive.'

**As State President, to a business
lunch in Johannesburg**
***The Star* 20 January 1986**

'I like the lighter side of life and I like to be with friends where I can have some laughter.'

**London *Sunday Times* Magazine
29 March 1987**

'Black friends? Well, up to a few years ago, on my brother's farm lived black people who were youngsters with me on my father's farm. And when they see me we behave in a natural way towards each other as we did when we were boys. We talk about old times and sometimes they question me on my present-day activities.'

London *Sunday Times* Magazine
29 March 1987

'The honour for this, one could almost call it a miracle, is due in particular to one man, Dr Verwoerd.'

As Minister of Housing, on handing the first completed house over to his department in the new White suburb of Triomf, built on the site of old black Sophiatown
***The Star* 6 September 1963**

'[He] represents the symbol of security of the country. We have come to say that we stand with you – because we stand with South Africa.'

On John Vorster's return from his European Tour as Prime Minister of SA 24 May 1977 (PW Botha was acting PM during this time)

'Dr Hertzog [leader of the HNP] is a political terrorist here in South Africa.'

As Minister of Defence, Pretoria NP meeting 10 March 1970

'[Dr Connie Mulder] has brought the greatest scandal the National Party has ever suffered. That is why he is where is.'

As Prime Minister, on former NP Minister
NP Meeting Cape Town
8 March 1980

'Let me tell, those who try to cause trouble in these ranks that between myself and the Minister of Public Works [Dr Andries Treurnicht] there are no differences in principle.'

As Prime Minister, on split in the NP
House of Assembly 21 March 1980

'They are always trying to get us apart. But I say to them! "try as you like, you will not get us apart".'

As Prime Minister, on rumours of his
secret plan to get rid of
Dr Treurnicht
Rustenburg 17 March 1981

'He [Dr Treurnicht] is a backstabber.'

**As Prime Minister – later declared
un-parliamentary by the Chairman
of Committee
House of Assembly
26 August 1983**

'You are a demolisher, a jackal and a hypocrite.'

**As Prime Minister, to Andries Treurnicht
House of Assembly
26 April 1984**

'The falling away of Dr Treurnicht will make no difference to the change of pace.'

**As Prime Minister, on SABC
14 March 1982**

'We don't think there is anything [Dr Treurnicht] can say that we need worry about.'

**As Prime Minister, on Treurnicht's
fears that his phone was bugged.
House of Assembly
1 February 1983**

'Tomorrow a man from Mars is coming here.'

**As Prime Minister, referring to
Andries Treurnicht's address the
next day to the CP
Louis Trichardt election meeting
4 May 1983**

'I think we should ignore them.'

**As Prime Minister, on Treurnicht and
the Conservative Party
House of Assembly
15 April 1982**

'I am appealing to Parliament. Protect yourselves against extra-parliamentary activities financed from abroad.'

**As State President,
House of Assembly
13 August 1987**

'Leave him [Eugene Terre'blanche leader of the AWB] to the Nats. Keep out of this battle − the Nats will take care of it.'

**As State President,
House of Assembly
28 April 1986**

'Perhaps we should not give these hotheads too much attention.'

**As Prime Minister, on the AWB
House of Assembly
15 April 1982**

'It is everybody's right to demonstrate and even to make a fool of themselves.'

**As Prime Minister, about demonstrations
during his European visit
Switzerland
31 May 1984**

'This is not the time for kindergarten politics.'

**As Prime Minister, Warrenton
24 July 1982**

'Even if you put your backside into a thornbush it [SA's multiracial society] will not change.'

**As Prime Minister, Nylstroom
18 November 1982**

'My friend, if they were all [sent to their homelands] who would bring you your coffee in the morning and you will probably need someone to change your nappy as well.'

**As Prime Minister,
to interjector at NP Meeting Koedoespoort
27 August 1979**

'Are you so degenerate that you are not even proud of what your country has achieved?'

**As Prime Minister, to a heckler
Durban
21 April 1981**

'I last heard those kind of sounds when I opened a cattle show.'

**As Prime Minister, to hecklers
Rustenburg
17 March 1981**

'We cannot speak at the same time. Has your husband not taught you that? Do you know what King Solomon said about a nagging wife? It's like the dripping of a tap.'

As Prime Minister, to the heckling leader of the *Kappiekommando* in Waterkloof at by-election meeting 27 April 1983

'I met the Honourable Member for Houghton's twin sister yesterday.'

As Prime Minister, referring to his spat with the leader of the *Kappiekommando* in Waterkloof House of Assembly 28 April 1983

'I cannot as leader of the Cape National Party approve of the use of tomatoes, eggs and other objects to disrupt the orderliness of meetings.'

Reacting to a rowdy HNP meeting in Paarl
The Star **13 November 1969**

'You don't have bad manners. You are just childish. You go home and think about how you should behave at future political meetings.'

As State President, to a questioner who suggested that his welcome in politics had been overstayed. Election meeting Stellenbosch 22 April 1987

'The fact that [hecklers] can shout at the Head of the Government of South Africa proves that we are a free country.'

As State President, Election meeting Pietermaritzburg 30 April 1987

'I grew up on a farm and we have an Afrikaans saying which goes: I can recognise a skunk by its smell.'

As State President, on negative advice
from so-called friends.
NP Congress Durban
15 August 1985

'The Progressive Party has throughout its history interceded for subversive elements in South Africa.'

As Minister of Defence,
House of Assembly
23 April 1975

'Hens will grow teeth before I introduce PFP policy.'

As Prime Minister,
House of Assembly
26 August 1981

'If the Opposition wish to help this Government as true South Africans, they can help our homelands policy to flourish.'

As Minister of Defence,
House of Assembly
24 January 1977

'All of us deep in our hearts have a little of the HNP in us. The liberals have more HNP than we do. They preach one thing and practice discrimination.'

As Prime Minister,
NP Congress Durban
20 August 1982

'This is the year in which sides will have to be taken.'

As State President, in a NP advert in
the press on the coming election
30 January 1987

'This election [of May 1987] is about the broadening of democracy and freedom. Voters must unite on May 6 for a vote of confidence in their security forces.'

**As State President,
Election meeting Johanesburg
4 May 1987**

'I have taken part in many elections without TV and have no great desire to be a film star.'

**As Prime Minister, on TV debates
Vereeniging election meeting
7 April 1981**

'Something worse could have hit the voters – I might have been singing on this record.'

**As State President, on receiving a copy
of the NP Election record
The Star 24 March 1987**

'Although the Government maintains the media regulations were necessary to maintain public order, public safety and to end the emergency, the Government believes that the election campaign must be marked by the greatest possible degree of free, open and recognisable discussion of participating parties and individual standpoints.'

As State President,
House of Assembly
4 February 1987

'I have never regarded myself as infallible or have never seen myself as the saviour of the nation.'

As Prime Minister, NP Congress Port Elizabeth reflecting as leader of the NP in the Cape. 30 September 1980

'To relax, to take my mind totally off things, I turn to my Bible which I read at least once a day.'

London *Sunday Times* Magazine 29 March 1987

'I can only withdraw myself for a few hours each day, that's all. As they say in the circus: the show must go on.'

As State President, *Rapport* 12 January 1986

'We must stop telling our people they are in such a bad state. South Africa is in a better state than any country in Africa.'

As State President,
House of Delegates
20 August 1987

'We fully realise that we do hold the key. We also know that the key can open the door to peaceful coexistence in multi-cultural countries worldwide. But there are elements obstructing us in using the key.'

As State President, on his meeting
with Sir Geoffrey Howe
Financial Mail 1 August 1986

'The government cannot think for adult citizens of this country.'

As State President,
House of Assembly
13 August 1987

'Effective meaningful education is possible only if politics are excluded from it.'

**As State President,
opening Parliament Cape Town
30 January 1987**

'Stop shouting at us; stop putting stumbling blocks in our way. There is a different, wiser approach to dealing with us.'

**As Prime Minister,
Press Conference prior to meeting the
five Foreign Ministers in Pretoria
19 October 1978**

'I am not prepared to lead White South Africans and other minority groups on the road to abdication and suicide.'

**As State President,
NP Congress Durban
15 August 1985**

'That which the public has the evident right to know, no authority should keep from it. Secrecy for the sake of secrecy, or to conceal incompetence and corruption, will not be tolerated by the government at any level of public administration.'

As State President,
House of Assembly
17 August 1987

'If civilization does triumph, we need have no fear for the future. If it does not there is no law that can possibly save us.'

As Prime Minister, Springbok
15 May 1982

'There is a new trek ahead of us, not into a gloom, but into a bright future for us all.'

As Prime Minister, at George
28 October 1978

'There is a beautiful side of South Africa also.'

As State President,
Election meeting Pietermaritzburg
30 April 1987

'Where is my wife?'

**First words spoken as Prime Minister
of South Africa on the steps of
Parliament Cape Town
28 September 1978**

'I'm not a good cook: my wife, Elize, says the only knowledge I have is knowing when water has come to the boil.'

**As State President,
London *Sunday Times* Magazine
29 March 1987**

'When you go to bed at night you can't go to bed with hatred in your heart because then you can't sleep. And I'm a good sleeper, ask my wife.'

**As Prime Minister,
The Star
28 September 1982**

'I switch off the lights and sleep within a few minutes. I never take a guilty conscience with me to bed.'

**London *Sunday Times* Magazine
29 March 1987**